wise me up®

TO COLD CALLING

wise me up®

TO COLD CALLING

Shea Heer

The Book Guild Ltd

First published in Great Britain in 2018 by
The Book Guild Ltd
9 Priory Business Park
Wistow Road, Kibworth
Leicestershire, LE8 0RX
Freephone: 0800 999 2982
www.bookguild.co.uk
Email: info@bookguild.co.uk
Twitter: @bookguild

Typeset in Aldine401 BT

Printed and bound in Great Britain by 4edge Limited

ISBN 978 1912575 619

British Library Cataloguing in Publication Data.
A catalogue record for this book is available from the British Library.

Printed on FSC accredited paper

To my partner, friend, love and greatest supporter of my work, Peter. I love you and thank you for your belief in my ability.

To my son, Reuben, I thank you for your patience.

To my YouTube subscribers and especially Preston King, who repeatedly asked me to write this book. Thank you.

CONTENTS

ABOUT THE AUTHOR

Shea discovered her passion and talent for selling whilst working in the family business. This is where she learned how connecting with the buyer creates results. Her career outside of the family started as a door-to-door salesperson selling cable phone and television services to the consumer. Against all odds in a male dominated world Shea became the most successful field saleswoman they have ever had and consistently achieved rewards as a top performer in the company.

Shea now has over 20 years of sales and sales training experience, including B2C, B2B, Field, Retail, and Telephone. She is CIPD[1] qualified, a Fellow of ISMM[2] and a certified business practitioner in NLP[3], holds an NEB[4] management certificate, has built and runs a sideline hospitality business and has a growing YouTube channel dedicated to helping sales professionals with everything from cold calling to negotiating.

---

1   Chartered Institute of Personnel & Development.
2   Institute of Sales & Marketing Management.
3   Neuro Linguistic Programming.
4   Institute of leadership and management.

She is also a happily divorced mum and now partner living in Gloucestershire, UK. Shea's personal values are:

1. Honesty is the key to respect and honour.
2. Optimism is the key to progress.
3. Risk is just another word for exploring.
4. Love is the key to sustainability.
5. Karma is real.

INTRODUCTION

I think cold calling is still as effective today as it ever has been and I believe that it can open plenty of doors for you if you know how to make the calls confidently. In this book I have identified what the fears are throughout a typical cold calling process and I have explained how you can eliminate them. I also share with you how you can get better results through understanding the impact of your behaviour so that you can control this to achieve what you want to on a call. My thoughts, ideas, tips and suggestions are based on over 20 years of experience in sales and sales training, coaching, receiving and making cold calls. This book challenges you to think about your approach and offers different ways to help you to be great in your own unique way. Don't try to be better by copying what other people do. This book will help you to be you, but be a better you.

"Being a good salesperson requires skills. Being a great salesperson requires an attitude to improve."

If you are a salesperson and you are reading this then you are already showing signs of being a great salesperson.

COLD CALLING – WHAT IS IT?

It's historically known as a numbers game with a sales script. To me it simply means a call that was not expected or not asked for by the recipient. Alternatively, some call it an unsolicited call. It does not mean aggressive, offensive or rude. In fact, I believe a cold call that is carried out well should not leave any of those thoughts in either the recipient's or the caller's mind during or after the call. So with my business being about helping salespeople I had to analyse why cold calling is such a challenge. After all, it is just a phone call and what's the worst that can happen?

> *"Turn cold calls into warm leads by making them and not fearing them!"*

ARE COLD CALLS NECESSARY?

There have been and still are many discussions or debates about how necessary it is to make cold calls. Some might think that in today's age of social media and marketing, cold calling is an unnecessary pest and might tarnish the sales profession. Some feel it is necessary as a direct approach. I am biased toward the latter, probably because of my background.

There have been countless examples of how a cold call can lead to a huge success. In today's world it seems like an old-fashioned way of selling though I believe cold calling is the most direct way of connecting with prospects. Direct marketing is probably more widely connected with and more easily understood by many as the terminology used to describe marketing emails or e-shots. This is interesting because whilst the intention of an email might very well be to go direct to the decision maker's inbox, we actually have little intelligence to tell us that the prospect has received or really read it. By this I don't mean to say that they clicked on it or moved it to a different file, I mean did they actually receive the message using the email address that the email was sent to and did they actually read the words in it.

Other alternatives to cold calling might be exhibiting or networking. This can be effective because you could say that you have a captive audience and one which is halfway ready to buy. It's more in line with retail where a customer comes to browse so the chances are that they are already receptive to the idea of that product or service category. However, it can be quite an expensive way to build business, especially if you are a start-up and don't have the funds to compete in the presence of the big corporates, who have experts working on their stands with big budgets.

Networking meetings are another way of finding new business, and again it can work. There is truth in six degrees of separation and sometimes it's about who you know, not just what you know. I think one of the reasons networking can be effective is that it's based on face-to-face interactions and face-to-face is proven to be highly effective in selling. The only downside of this is that it can be a lengthy, time-consuming process to get to the golden opportunity and it means having to physically travel to places and sometimes even pay to attend the events. In fact, some events like the people summits cost thousands of pounds to attend. I always find that networkers are lovely people who genuinely want to help others but they also have to focus on building their own business. Some people are great at this and manage to open lots of doors through networking but it's not everyone's cup of tea especially if you don't have the time and budget.

Some people argue that they don't need to cold call because you can work through social media, networking and referrals. I've actually seen such comments on LinkedIn. If that works for them then that's great as it probably fits with their style of business and again this all depends on how long you have to gain traction and recognition through these sites. Social media today has become as aggressive a selling platform as email marketing and as there are now so many of them I can imagine that only selective posts are actually read anymore. We also all know that some posts that are consistent with lots of content could be written by profile owner's social media representative so any incoming responses might still be filtered by the writer acting as a gatekeeper. I think it's good to bear in mind that everyone on social media is in the main present on the sites to sell either themselves or a business, product, service or concept or even a brand.

So I am biased to thinking that cold calling is one of the most effective ways in which to reach out, make contact and qualify if there's any opportunity there and if there is, to then understand what you have to do to win it. Here's an example of one of my earliest cold calling successes since starting this business.

It was late 2008 and the financial world was a mess! A well-known American financial services firm took a dive and brought many a financial institution down with them. The ripple effects were big and hit just about all industries. Company purse strings were tightened to make plans for uncertain trading and to focus on survival strategies. Here was little old me sitting in my newly refurbished loft thinking about nothing other than making my brand new training business work. To be honest, I paid little attention to the news after the first few weeks of havoc had hit the headlines. I just knew I had to find some business. I had already done some research-related calls to local businesses to find out what was important to them at this time. 'Sales' were still high on the agenda. Funny because everyone I spoke to in business said that they needed to stop buying but start selling more. How does that work? Anyway, what better time to position myself, and what a great opportunity to rival the larger and more costly sales training companies who had overheads to pay. I had already spent time working in a sales training consultancy who hired freelancers so I knew how it worked. With this knowledge I was ready to take on any objection the climate could throw at me. I was prepared. I had thought about how I can respond so that my answers would demonstrate how I can help potential customers rather than be beaten into defending my position. When I talk more about objections later in this book I'll expand on this.

So I used my understanding of what people wanted from me to be able to get through the door of some of the largest businesses I was fortunate enough to work with in that first year. One of them is a leading European construction group who was looking to enhance sales but didn't want to pay the costs they had already been paying to their current training provider. Their training provider was a leading training consultancy here in the UK with a great reputation. I made a random cold call to this builders' merchant and on speaking to the HR manager I was able to secure an appointment to meet them. Their need was for more effective sales techniques to battle the financial climate, and the objection was cost. I showed how I could add value through providing them with the expertise and depth of sales training knowledge that they were looking for but as I don't have the overheads that they are used to paying, I could give them real cost-effective solutions that would be totally bespoke to them. With this company we agreed solutions and delivered training for a number of years, expanding across other brands within the group.

I opened and closed at least three other major opportunities in those opening months and lots since the start of my business just through cold calling. There were no leads; I simply found the main head office numbers and dialled them, got through to the relevant influencer or decision maker, made an appointment and then won the business through a meeting followed by a proposal followed by a close. There was no rocket science involved throughout. It was simply a series of interactions with professionals who also happen to be human beings with a problem to be solved and a reputation to maintain. So no matter what people say about cold calling, I believe it works!

"Selling is an art and I am a great artist!"

DOORS & LOCKS

If we think of cold calling as being all about opening doors then in order to open those doors with customers I believe you have to first unlock them in your own mind. Doors are opened through interactions; locks are unlocked through the mind. By locks, I'm referring to the mental fears which inhibit success. I have observed so many cold callers and one of the common tell-tale behaviours of fear is when a salesperson is ready to come off a call before the gatekeeper. Think about it. If you were to analyse any of your most recent calls you really have to be honest about whether you were the first to come away from that call, and were you assertive enough or did you just give up too early? This can be hard to self-assess; admittedly, it's easier and more effective for me as a coach to work with you on this because there are a few variables or considerations you have to give to each situation. Let me explain this in stages. First, I should explain what I believe to be the doors and locks.

Sometimes it's not the skills that a cold caller lacks when making a call, it's your own inhibitions to making the call which can be your downfall. No amount of skill will get you beyond any door if you are not mentally prepared. By being mentally prepared I mean being able to eliminate any fears from your mind. The fears will lock you out before you even get a chance to work your way through the door. What happens is that people go ahead and start cold calling but don't get through any door because they haven't unlocked the fear that stands in their way. I want to show you how to unlock your fears that stand in front of the door so you can then apply your skill positively and get through each door.

So what are the locks that you have to unlock before you get through the doors on a cold call? First, you should understand what the doors are, then the locks.

The Door to the next stage	The Lock (fear)
1. First Impressions	Fear of rejection
2. Objections	Losing control
3. The Decision Maker	Verbal diarrhoea

Door 1: First hurdle is to be liked immediately. The lock therefore (fear) = Fear of being rejected.

Door 2: The objections that you know you will have to face and how they can throw you off guard and lose you control of the conversation.

Door 3: This is the one chance you have to impress the decision maker, so the fear is that you don't mess it up with what you say.

There is another fear that I want to just mention before I talk about the three locks above. This fear relates more to people who work in an open-plan call centre and only applies to the less experienced salespeople and this one is about being 'heard'.

I have coached a number of people and in my opinion it is usually the new or less experienced people, and when I say experience it could simply be the time spent working in an open-plan environment as opposed to experience in sales. For example, I have met with experienced salespeople who had worked from home but when put into an open-plan sales environment they used to clam up. This fear is not about the interaction with the customer so much but more about the sales person's ego. Now before we start thinking about big heads and show off attitudes, let's just understand that an ego is simply the conscious part of the person's mind. Their consciousness of how they want to be seen as a person. So when I use the term 'ego' I use it in its truest form. For example, I am talking about people who care about 'getting it right' in front of their peers and managers. Also, people who don't want to sound 'silly'. The salespeople in this category are usually very nice normal people who are loyal and genuine in their intent. They just can't get used to being in an environment in which people might be listening to them.

I recently had a reasonably long telephone conversation with someone who sat in this category of person. He is a really nice young man who desperately wanted to do well. He reached out to me and through conversation he told me that one of his biggest put-offs was the fact that other people in the open-plan office could hear what he was saying which made him really self-conscious and so we discussed how this was inhibiting him from coming across the way he wanted to come across on his calls. We talked for quite a while, and during that time he was laying his fears out to me on the phone and being really honest about his skills gaps or areas he wanted to develop. Also, during the whole of that call time, he was actually travelling about in public including on public transport. At the end of the call I said to him, "You have been talking to me very openly about yourself, your sales ability and your fears on the phone while travelling in public." He was a little quiet and then said "yes" not knowing where I was leading to, and so I replied, "Did you at any point during that call think that others around you might be listening to you, hearing what you are saying and making judgements about you?" He thought for a moment before saying "no, I actually never thought about it". I explored it further with him encouraging him to realise that when he is confident about what he is saying and more importantly when he is focussed on the person he is talking to, he will be able to drop the fear of people around him hearing what he's saying. A good number of strangers he sat next to or walked by will have heard parts of his conversation to me on the phone but none of it occurred to him. He was 'in the call'. When he was speaking to me he knew what he wanted to say and more importantly he was fixed on getting the answers he wanted from me. So I explained that if he was to treat his cold calls in the same way that he did the call with me he could easily overcome that fear. All he had to do was:

"Be in the call, not in the room."

Sometimes in a very target-driven call centre it can be hard to be in the call because of the pressure of time spent on calls, but if this is where you are then it's more a high pressure numbers game and not a customer-focussed operation.

Another thing that's useful to think about here is that if colleagues listen to you and then you listen to them, I would bet that you can hear those colleagues saying words or phrases they might have picked up from you. In the same way it's always good to hear what they are saying because you can pinch new and effective phrases or approaches from them.

"Stealing is legal in learning."

There is a buzz about being in a sales office and it can be really enjoyable.

DOOR 1

FIRST IMPRESSIONS

LOCK 1 – FEAR OF REJECTION

Rejection is a fear that we all have to some degree, some more than others, though I would bet that most sales professionals are good with people and will be emotive enough to care whether they are liked or not. This means we will have a fear of rejection and cold calling is all about being able to deal with it. It's quite normal to feel this fear, and doesn't mean that you are weak or any less than someone who pretends not to fear rejection, you just need to learn how to overcome it. For this I believe you have to approach the call so that you are immediately liked by the person or people on the other end of the line. That could be the gatekeeper at first and then the decision maker afterwards. It would be naïve to think that just because you got the gatekeeper to like you that the decision maker will also automatically like you, so being liked over the phone is a skill that can serve you well. We are talking about rapport. I'm sure this is a familiar word to you. If they like what they hear they will make a decision on you. If what you say resonates positively with them then they will like you, and if you sing off the same page you will be in rapport and so the first door will open up. Sounds easier than it is, not, but then that's why I'm writing about it.

"Would you listen to you?"

This is a question that I will always ask all my delegates when on this subject. I also explain that when you ask yourself that question if you hesitate to answer then it's time to change what you say or the way in which you say it. However, you have to be able to hear what you are saying first. Stop and think about how you approach your calls maybe even say it in the mirror and then think to yourself – "would I listen to me? Do I sound good enough for me to want to carry on listening to myself beyond the first line of my introduction?" To really understand how you come across you have to be able to put yourself in the listener's position.

I'm sure we all or at least most of us know what it's like to be on the receiving end of a sales call and from what I have learned from many people is that there are few occasions when we actually give time to listen to the caller, especially when they are calling you at home. We can't eliminate what I think is a general negative preconception about cold callers, but we can make this preconceived thought work in our favour, just like I did when I used the economic climate to my advantage to get in front of customers when I first set up my business. Consider your own experiences and also what you have heard from other people, friends and family. You can think about what people don't want to hear, in other words the reasons why cold callers are disliked and do the opposite. What words would you associate with a negative cold call? Then think about how you can alter what you say and do, to make sure you eliminate these from the interaction.

For example, I always think about how people use the word 'pushy' for salespeople and they use it in a very negative way. So as a cold caller you have to breakdown what you think would make the recipient of a call describe the caller as being pushy. My understanding from my research is that 'pushy' is a caller whose volume is loud, they don't stop talking and they don't listen to what you're saying. They railroad and just tell, tell, tell.

"Telling is not selling."

I don't personally believe that these types of aggressive calls are always down to the caller themselves. Some are but not all. I think pressure on some of them to sell may have promoted certain behaviours. Companies will often recruit people who don't have the skill and with all good intentions aim to train them to be 'great' salespeople. The word 'great' here has to be understood fully. What I call a 'great' sales person might not be what others agree is a 'great' salesperson. The level of 'great' in call centres might mainly be measured by quantities of sales and not quality of sales. With quantity being the objective, pressure to sell can lead to behaviours that don't align to quality. I believe selling is an art and you can't put pressure on an artist if you want the best from them.

Years ago I started my professional selling career knocking on doors. These were cold calls but on foot and face-to-face. In the five years I spent doing this I only really came across a handful of people who were verbally aggressive toward me and never physically. However, if I analyse five years of cold calling I can say that for me the ratio of pleasant to unpleasant encounters is quite different on the phone. I have experienced far more unpleasant encounters over the phone.

It has been proven that we humans take more kindly to face-to-face interactions than any other. We judge a message being conveyed mostly and primarily on the body language that accompanies the verbal tone and content. So if cold calling is not face-to-face we take away the most impactful communication tool that we have. I have always taught my delegates to take part in exercises where vision is taken out of the equation and realise the importance of what they hear. Or if they know someone who is blind they might already know the answer to this. Not being able to see anything amplifies what you hear, i.e. the tone and words are amplified when we have no body language. They become far more important. So now the recipient of a message on the phone will judge the message they hear on the tone and words used. You could say that now your tone and words matter twice as much without body language. That being said, I still believe there is an element of body language that still dictates the mood of the call. It all starts with the mind and how you think as this will dictate your mood; your mood will then be reflected in your natural body language (which you may not even be aware of), and your body language will typically influence your tone on the phone. For example, someone sitting slouched and appearing to be unhappy will not be able to convey a positive and energetic tone. They may think they can but the recipient probably hears something else. The body language is so primitive and dominant that it can influence your tone, and the words used will be judged on that tone. Hence, it is important, as Albert Mehrabian (1) said, to keep your non-verbal and verbal content congruent. If you want to come across enthusiastic then first you have to think enthusiastically about what you are doing. If you want your recipient to believe in what you are saying then you have to believe in what you are saying and say what you believe in a believable way. A classic example of when callers are not congruent in communication is when they are reading a script. We can always tell when a person is not connecting with the words because we read into it with what's called our primate or more widely known as our 'gut' instinct. It is also one reason why many callers lose their customer early on in a call. So ask yourself:

"Would you listen to you?"

After a few calls that have not in your opinion been successful calls perhaps think about how you might be being perceived. Are you being honest? Despite the stigmas attached to sales, great cold callers are not good at lying and nor are they good at being pushy. What they are good at is to recognise how they come across and at being receptive to change. A great salesperson asks themselves the question "would I listen to me?" and they will recognise when to change what they are saying and how they are saying it.

If you are unwilling to do this you might easily fall into a category of people who believe their calls are not being answered or are not successful because of factors outside of your own control. If this happens you have just locked yourself out. Try this:

FRESH is an acronym but is relevant to first impressions. I always think that you have to try to stand out from the crowd. Be different. The person you are about to call may have had many callers in their day so aim to be the one that is different or in other words be FRESH. I came across this acronym years ago and it's a really good way of reminding yourself of its importance to your call. This acronym is one you can create for yourself. All you have to do is put a word that starts with each letter, next to that letter. Each word you choose should say how you want to come across on the phone. One example for F might be Friendly. Have a go, make it your personal one. What is your FRESH?

Friendly
R
E
S
H

"It's wise to be in the other person's shoes not one step ahead of them."

In one or two of my YouTube videos you might see me coming away from a call having acknowledged that the gatekeeper was busy and so they didn't come across too friendly. I could hear the gatekeeper's other phone ringing and their tone beginning to get stressed. Now I could have stayed on that phone and been persistent about my objective but I didn't want to lose any future relations with them. So I politely acknowledged what I heard and asked if they'd rather I call in a short while when they have had chance to breathe. People will appreciate the fact that you acknowledge them and their challenges. You might come across as a breath of fresh air because you actually put them and their needs first rather than try to ram your own agenda down their throat. You will be especially appreciated by the people who have to deal with callers all day long. Besides, if you catch them in that kind of mood you might end up in conflict and blow the opportunity. Remember they are people not machines and they certainly don't want or mean to be hostile. That moment when you call them could be the worst or best part of their day and your approach might just be the decider on that one. So ask yourself, what kind of impression would you want to leave on that person?

This doesn't just work with the gatekeeper it's equally important to acknowledge when you have called a decision maker at a less convenient time. Time is precious to everyone especially you the salesperson, as

I'm sure you're already aware. Quite often I hear sales people talking about the decision maker's time and yet not much about their own time as if their own doesn't count. What tends to work for me is that on every call I keep my focus on making each call worth my time, and I automatically get better results. It works! You will stop worrying about time altogether and find yourself thinking more about getting what you can out of the call. Try having a piece of paper in front of you with the words, "make it worth my time?" written on it. This will motivate you to find out more about who you are speaking to and hence learn more about the opportunity.

RAPPORT

Whether you are a B2B caller or a B2C caller you will need to win the trust of your recipient straight away. That first impression does count. So when you read from a script that you don't connect with you will come across, as I mentioned above, as non-congruent so a person listening to you can't take to you as easily. I secretly put names to the different types of callers who fail to build a rapport because of their initial approach. Let me share:

The undercover caller

I had a caller once tell me his name was Jacob. Totally believable except something told me that this young foreign voice didn't belong to a Jacob. Having had first-hand experience of coaching sales managers in overseas call centres I knew that this young caller was probably working to a guideline provided by a trainer or coach. I can see why the callers are asked to do this. They will have been told to "make your name easy to pronounce for your target market" so that the person they call can relate to them better. I however have to challenge that theory. If I know the person has just lied to me about their name, how do I believe anything else that comes from this person is credible? Hence, there will be no further time for rapport. My defences were up straight away. I did not hang up. I simply asked a few questions. Here's how it went:

"Is your name really Jacob?"
"Yes madam," (Indian accent)
"Where are you from then Jacob?"
"I am calling from… (company name)"
"No, sorry, I mean where in the world are you located right now?"
"Madam, I am calling you from England."
"Really? Where in England?"

Phone goes down. I should point out that the caller put the phone down in frustration. They hadn't really expected such responses.

So that was an example of how a caller can lose their recipient early by something as simple as a false name and simply not being honest. That person might have been the most genuine hard working soldier in that call centre but given a script and guided to lie on it made it impossible for him to build a rapport. You might think that I only felt that way because I have that inside knowledge. Well this might be true but I have also listened to the reactions of the call recipients where the caller is immediately challenged with questions such as "where are you calling from?"; this is a sure sign of suspicion.

That was a B2C call but it happens in B2B calls too. A classic example:

> *"Hi, my name is… I'm calling on behalf of (big mobile phone company) to see if we can find a better business plan for your mobile phone."*

This caller called me about 6 months ago. They used the name of my current mobile or cell provider. By doing so, their plan would be to engage me straight away with the knowledge that this call is from someone I already trust.

This poor young lady spent about 30 minutes going through everything with me on tariffs and bundles and prices and extras, not once asking me if I would be willing to change from my current provider. Why? Because the theory for them is that my main concern like everyone else will be to lower my costs on my plan. Well this might be partly right but I'm more concerned about coverage and roaming support. What happened here was that the caller had already decided what I wanted without asking me. Their focus remained on price or tariffs and as a result she wasted 35 minutes of her own time. Mine was well spent because I was using her call to educate myself on call habits. So I was happy. However, she wasn't so happy when the end of the call went like this:

"So, Mrs Heer shall I go ahead and set that up for you?"
"Wait, remind me where you are from again."
To which she replied with her employing company name.
"So you don't work for… (my mobile provider)?"
"No."
"So, you want me to change provider for this?"
"Yes, but you would be paying less for…"
"OK, I understand that but I'm afraid I'm not prepared to change provider. I'm really sorry. Perhaps if you had made it clear that you would be searching for other providers to better my call plans then I would have saved you 30 minutes of your time."

She hung up.

I had another 2 calls from 2 more different agents from that same office within a month of each other who used the same approach, so I can only imagine that this is what they are being coached to say and I have to disagree with it. It simply does not pay to be deceitful or, as I call it, to put the truth or detail undercover. Say why you are calling and save yourself valuable time by being upfront about what you want to do for the person you are calling.

"Find out what's important to them not what you think is important to them."

Another example of an undercover caller, as I can't resist this one. It's a very common one:

"Is this a cold call?"
"No, not really…"

Salespeople will try to make up all sorts of answers to this simple question for fear of not getting past the gatekeeper. Well actually as soon as you start to fumble about or avoid the question or say "no it isn't" in any way then the recipient will feel an uneasiness about you. They may put you through but they themselves have already formed an opinion which will be something like "really!?"

I find honesty is one of the easiest and most effective values to have when selling. It means you don't have to try to find a clever way of covering up who you are and why you are calling.

The truth builds rapport. I've had so many cold callers who tend to beat around the bush before getting to the point. I mean fumbling around for clever ways to find out if you would be interested in something. I've experienced the undercover salesperson many times. Let me give you another example of what I mean by this; salesperson wants to sell something that they believe will benefit me:

"I'm calling you because you qualify for an opportunity to…"

My immediate thoughts: Err what? Qualify? What gives the salesperson the right to place a judgement on me? 'Qualify' is a dangerous way of approaching prospective customers. I understand why salespeople might have been encouraged to use this approach because through proven studies and research, theories lead us to believe that people are motivated by achievement and recognition. So it would seem to make sense to tell someone they qualified for something. You might think this will open them up, make them feel positive and motivated but recognition and achievement means more to us when it is recognised by someone we have respect for, not a stranger. When it is delivered by a stranger we might feel somewhat belittled or suspicious. The question 'what's the catch?' comes to mind. We're all different and according to the same studies we will respond slightly differently. Some might challenge the statement with something like "really? I don't remember entering any kind of competition…". Some might react by being totally defensive: "you don't know anything about me…". Others might silently continue to listen but be totally guarded and not say anything till you finish. They hang up. There might be a few people who react positively to this statement and I do mean just a few. However, I think the underlying question of trust will still be at large. So why would you want to say something that diluted your chances of having a meaningful conversation with the recipient?

The submissive caller

This is the caller who puts themselves in an inferior position through the language and tone that they use with their prospects. At the same time you will automatically put the prospect into a superior position. According to the theory of transactional analysis (2) you could be putting yourself into what is called a 'child' mind-set and then the other person, in this case your prospect, automatically takes on the 'parent' role. So you will be talked down to from that moment onward in a parental fashion that could be condescending, maternal, or simply directive, but their responses are simply a reaction to the positions that you will have created through your choice of language and tone.

Many salespeople put themselves in a submissive position with their prospects on the phone. Having put much thought into why and understanding salespeople, I have worked out that this happens because there is a fine line between behaviour that is perceived as being polite and that which gives a perception of you being submissive. Thus, if you don't know when being polite crosses over to being submissive, then you can't really control it. So let's recognise some of the language, tone and approaches that are polite vs those that put you in a submissive position:

"Don't be sorry, be strong."

A great and most known apologetic word is 'sorry'. It is polite but when used in conjunction with phrases like "sorry to disturb you", it becomes submissive. If you are sorry to disturb them, then why are you on the phone calling them? Also, if you start off by being sorry for calling them, what chance have you got to continue the call, be in control of the call and then achieve your objective?

There is nothing wrong with using the word in empathy to what you hear, such as "well, I'm sorry to hear that" or when you use it to ask the other person to repeat what they said: "sorry, could you say that again…". Unfortunately, it does become submissive when you are apologising for your action toward them.

If you are still in the habit of apologising for calling think about what I said. Remember you have a legitimate reason to call so don't be apologetic about it, don't be afraid to say who you are and why you are calling. Be confident and use your time wisely. Get what you can from them while you can. This is a moment that can make or break your opportunity so don't lose it by being 'sorry' for calling them.

Apart from the obvious sentences like "sorry to disturb you", there are other ways in which you can still put yourself that submissive position. How you address someone can also have the same reaction.

'Mrs, Mr, Sir, Madam' are all words that might cross over to suggest you are putting the prospect in a superior position. I say 'might' because in some parts of the world it could be a cultural behaviour in which case I wouldn't expect you change it. However, in places where you know that it is common practice to address the market by the first name then why would you want to put a formal barrier between you and your prospect? If you have their name why not use it? We are no longer in the days where we have to address our seniors by their surname and nor are we serving in an institute. There are times when I haven't even used a surname to ask for the decision maker.

Sometimes it's not the words you use, it's just the tone. A fast racy pace always tells me that you just want to get it over and done with. Volume should be as strong as theirs. To avoid putting yourself in the submissive position it is so vital that you mirror your tone to theirs. Sometimes it's hard to hear people over the phone so if you talk really quietly make sure they can hear you when you're on the phone.

Be careful of too much hesitation and rushing in. All these are signs of a lack of confidence giving the prospect the opportunity to take control of your call.

The generous caller

"Hi, we've recently conducted a survey of small businesses to see how we can help them to grow and I'm calling you to offer you a free…"

Now we are all hard-wired to believe that nobody gets anything for free. The immediate question that springs to mind when we see or hear the word free is "what's the catch?"

Every single time you ask that question, the sales person's whole confidence breaks down and becomes defensive. "There is no catch" they will say followed by "all we ask is that you…"

Now all of this is still widely used in some industries such as the time-share industry where everything is about hard selling but in the world of professional selling in B2B it's important to refrain from using trigger words such as 'free'. Let's face it, if you want to offer something for no extra cost, then you are giving away extra value add-ons. These should strictly be used for negotiation purposes. Free giveaways are a sign of desperation and low value services or products. If you want to sell something of real value then you have to believe in the value you are selling.

Recently I spoke to a young man who has just started a business where he was offering a part of his service under the heading of 'free'. The service he offered was a 'free survey'. I was coaching him and we discussed this. After a conversation about the perception that the word free gives, he agreed that he would rephrase his offering to say this: "one of the reasons we believe we offer great value is that we also conduct a full survey…" The young man immediately understood how the two sentences (the one he used to say to prospects and this latter one I coached him toward) gave two completely different perceptions of his company and his status in the market place. Needless to say, he no longer associates his offering with the word 'free'.

"Everything we give requires effort. We just have to recognise the value of what we give."

CONVERSATIONS

In my opinion, cold calls should be made of two-way conversations. This can be achieved with the use of questions. In the first instance the questions are to help you to get through to the right person and to make sure you are asking the right questions to the right person. After that, your questions will be more about understanding how you can position your product or service so as to get the best responses and all the while you will be able to keep the person on the call for longer giving you more opportunity to build an interest.

I've heard questions from both receiving cold calls from salespeople and from training salespeople. Here are some of the most popular ones. By popular I don't mean favourable, I mean most often heard or asked:

"Is this a good time to talk?"

This is an interesting one. Many people believe that we shouldn't ask this because it gives the decision maker a get-out clause. Others think they should ask because it's polite and comes across as respectful. I have to sit in the polite camp on this but I also agree with the people who say that this is not a good question to ask. Well it is good to ask in principle if you've caught them at a good time because you actually want to make the most of this opportunity without feeling you have to rush it and lose control of the conversation. However, I think there are more effective and less effective ways of asking the same question. Have a look at this and see what you think.

When coaching this I have to help my delegates to put themselves in the customer's headspace because to make a good judgement you really have to put your consumer head on. Be the buyer for a minute and think about which you believe sounds most effective. Remember we are looking to find a way of asking the prospect for their time whilst also being respectful of theirs and whilst trying to gauge their level of interest:

a. *"Is this a good time to talk?"*
b. *"I just want to discuss… if you have a couple of minutes?"*
c. *"I'm calling to discuss… May I carry on?"*

So what do you think? Try to think this through before you skip to what I think.

Consider this:

Look for assertiveness, confidence, respectfulness and sincerity.

Are there any words that might be taken in the wrong context?

Hopefully, you are thinking that any of these can work but it really depends on where in the conversation they come up and what surrounds the question.

As I always say to my delegates, there is no right or wrong when it comes to working in agreement with people, it's more about understanding, perception and control. You have to be able to understand how they might perceive what is being said and then control the flow of the conversation so that you remain on track and in favour.

These questions can each be effective when used in context but you have to recognise the context. Let's see if I can explain.

Example 'a' to me is asking if this is a good time to talk, which is interesting because they just took your call. So you might agree when some say that this question is risky as you might be giving them a get-out clause. You should also consider how you might feel at this point as the buyer. Here's my reaction to a recent such call:

"What's it about first?"

If your recipient is not aware of what you want two minutes for then the natural response would be to stop you in your tracks and challenge you on why they should give you two minutes. I'm sure you would agree. This then leads you straight into handling a question otherwise seen as an objection and all that rehearsed spiel is lost because you haven't been able to initiate a conversation.

Also, what does a 'good time' mean? Is there ever a 'good time' in today's world of 'I need it yesterday'? The fact is that there is no defined question in this other than a perception of what 'good time' is. You can't really judge what a good time to talk is unless you are clear of what tangible gain you will have from investing this time. That would mean it can be quite dependent upon how familiar they already are with your type of proposition. For example, I have received many calls from IT people who are speaking to the decision maker, i.e. me, but tend to speak in IT jargon which I don't understand so my natural instinct would be to say I have no time to listen further just now. This response will come in guises such as "I'm actually in the middle of something just now…" or "I'm really sorry I don't have the time for this just now…" or even the challenging response as mentioned earlier "why what is it about?" or "what exactly are you looking to sell to me?"

Example 'b' is the same question worded differently but more importantly it is also structured differently in that it comes in after the explanation. For this to be really effective it is important to make that opening line valuable and relevant. So for example, I would use it like this:

> *"Hi Helen, my name is Shea, my company specialises in bespoke sales training and I just wanted to take a couple minutes to understand where you might be with your training plan just now. Do you have anything in place as yet?"*

So you see how I have introduced myself and said Why I'm calling and then launched into my first question which puts me firmly in control of my call and have a conversation aligned to my planned structure. From here I will direct the conversation according to the answer I get from my listener. Automatically, I always feel really comfortable when this happens as I'm not waiting for the dreaded question "why are you calling?", I've already pre-eliminated it.

Example 'c' is a direct yet very respectful way of diverting control of the conversation to them but actually you still have it. So you are putting them in the driving seat to keep the conversation going. This is great because it's a closed question and most people will not feel comfortable and professional to just say "no". Think about it. How do you think you would sound if you just said one word "no" as a professional? I'm not saying it can't happen, I'm saying that "no" is a much harder word to deliver as a one-word answer than "yes". In the same way that it's harder to deliver bad news than good. Our fascination for bad news is because the negative form is quite alien to our natural mind. We have to train our brains to get used to it. So with this in mind the questions in example 'c' will invite them to either say why it's not appropriate for you to carry on at this point, or they will let you carry on. If they don't want you to carry on they will give a reason and that's something that could be valuable information for next time you call, e.g.:

"You can carry on but we have no budget for this till quarter three, so it might be more relevant for you to call me back then…"

This is not a bad answer; you just qualified enough to manage your cold calling time better.

The question in example 'c' is a closed question but in this context it works more as a leading question and leads the prospect to explain their position. Here's an example of how I mean:

"Hi Alice, I'm calling to see where you might be with marketing for this year. May I carry on?"

Alice: "Yes, but we have recently just budgeted for the year and I'm not sure we have room for any more right now."

So whilst her answer is allowing me to carry on, she has given me enough to understand the situation so I can tailor the next part of my pitch to be more relevant to her situation.

An alternative response:

"Actually I think I should stop you there because we have just had to put everything on hold for now as we are…"

Whatever answer you get with this one, the likelihood is that the response will invite more than a one-word answer and give you just a little more which will in turn help you to maintain control of the conversation so that you can either qualify further, sell to them, or recognise that you might be wasting your time this year.

Another great question:

"How are you today?"

This is a nice question to ask but again much like the "have you got time to talk" it's a question that can be ill-timed in your opening pitch. Think about how you feel when someone who you don't know asks you that question. I know that my immediate reaction is and will always be "I'm good thanks, what is the call about?". This is because I don't know the caller and I sense a stall for time and a break in this opening sentence big enough for me to take control of the call.

In cold calling it is essential that you maintain control of your call. After all, it is *your* call. You made it with good reason, so everything you say and any questions you ask should be prepared and timed in such a way that you maintain control. Here's a summary of what I believe are questions that show you are in control vs questions that can lose you control because of the response that they trigger in people.

Questions that ensure you maintain control	Questions that can lose you control
Who do you currently use for…?	How are you today? (Too soon to ask a personal question)
Do you have a budget in place for something like this?	Is it OK if I…? (Don't ask permission; you called to tell them about)
Can we go over a few things to see if there is any value in this for you?	Is this a good time? (Making it easy for them to get out of the call)
Are you the best person to speak to about…?	Would you like to know about…? (Too submissive)
Who is the best person to speak to about…?	Can I show you how to save money? (Assumptive on their need)
Have you considered other providers for? Is there any particular reason for…?	How would you like to save money? (Assumptive on their need)
When was the last time you looked at the market for this…?	
What's the most important factor about…. for you?	

You may have worked out that questions that are effective and help you maintain control are also those that follow your whole introduction, i.e. after you have stated why you are calling!

QUALIFYING QUESTIONS

You will see that the questions in the left column are all questions that will help you to maintain control of the call and also help you to maintain control of the call and also help you to identify how much potential there might be with this prospect for you or they can be questions that lead you to understand more about the people you are calling as a business. Questions on the right are examples of questions that can lose you control and ones that I think should be avoided due to the responses they trigger. The responses they trigger will cause you a challenge that you don't need.

Just to expand a little; the good questions to ask on a cold call are the ones that I call or refer to as 'qualifying questions' because they help you to identify how big an opportunity there is for you and in some cases the potential for you too. Having questions at the ready is an important part of effective cold calling. If the decision maker is not available to speak to immediately, questions like these give you an opportunity to build a rapport with the gatekeeper or other colleague that you might be talking to on the phone. More importantly for you, it helps you to understand who you are calling so that when you call back you have already turned the call from cold to warm making it an easier conversation to have. Remember what I said about making the call worth it. Just because the person who you have on your calling list is not available, it doesn't mean you can't gather valuable information and make sure that this call makes your next step smarter. So try to stay on the phone to get as many of your qualifying questions answered. It's all too easy for cold callers to put the phone down before the other person does. One person I was coaching was so desperate to come off the phone that although their tone was still very pleasant they leaned forward bringing the hand piece closer to the telephone base ready to hang up. As if there was a timer on how quickly they would be able to hang up after the last word. I thought it quite comical to watch as did the person I was coaching when I explained it to them. They really didn't realise that they were doing this.

LANGUAGE

"Words come easy, understanding takes effort."

As well as having good questions to ask it's also important to use universal language so you can be easily understood. I suppose it's just too easy these days to fall into jargon. A couple of times earlier I have mentioned the importance of clarity of your opening line or your opening gambit. Some might call it your 'elevator pitch'. What you call it really doesn't matter but what you put in it does. So put in conjunction with what I said earlier about perception and understanding, there are some things that you might want to think twice about regards your opening approach with reference to your language and tone.

To help me make my point I often use text like this one:

> *Hello, thanks for accepting my connect request. I just want to introduce myself and my business with you. We are expert in the following:- A). Website Development (Magento, PHP, .Net, Java, Wordpress, CMS… etc) B). Custom web design, – Static website design,Web portal design C). E-Commerce Solutions & Responsive Websites D). App Development (iPhone, iPad + Android) Please contact me back if you are interested in any service. Would be really happy to hear from you soon. Best Regards, Name.*

I received this message via LinkedIn. So you might think that this wouldn't happen on a call. Sadly, I have received cold calls which sound just like the written message above. It probably seems hard to believe but the question you should be asking yourself is, how often have you analysed the words in your opening approach? If you are finding it hard to get through to people then it could simply be that the words you are using are so industry specific that the other person has no idea what you are calling for and so they might find it easier to make excuses to get you off the line.

I have had salespeople call me and throw lots of IT

terms at me then actually expect me to respond. Here let me take you through one;

> *"Hi, is this Shea?" (actually they often use my surname but I don't like it so if you want to cold call me, call me by my first name please)*
> *"Yes, it is."*
> *"… I had a look at your website and I would like to talk to you about jargon, jargon, jargon…"*
> *"I'm sorry I am not very IT literate so you'll have to explain to me what exactly are you looking to sell to me?"*
> *"I want to see if you are interested in jargon, jargon, jargon."*
> *"I'm sorry I probably do need to think about whatever it is you are offering but I don't have the time right now, try again later or better still send me something on email."*

Any of this sound familiar? You'll see how I can't even recall the words they use. I don't remember because I didn't understand it. I didn't understand it so I don't really know if it might benefit me. I would like to be honest with the salesperson but I have nothing to respond to. There was hardly anything there that made sense to me.

So my tip to you on language would be to make it plain and simple for everyone to be able to understand. If someone has to work hard to understand what you are saying, you might not be someone they want to listen to anymore. Life's hard enough without you confusing it even more. Anyway, isn't what you are offering about relieving someone of a pressure or stress?

Let me explain this without complicating and making it long-winded. Tone is simply the way in which you express your words and therefore giving meaning to words for the listener. A great example to use for this is the word 'sorry'. You know when someone means it not by the word but by the way they say it. That's their tone you are reading. I can think of times I have challenged the person's sincerity when the word was delivered to me because I get a 'feeling' that the person didn't really mean it. That judgement I made is based on the person's tone. I'm sure you will have had similar experiences, where you might come away from a call and think "hmm, not sure if they really meant what they said". So remember that people will make judgements on you based on your tone. It's made up of your pace, pitch and volume all working together to create a rhythm that complements the words you are saying. I would never suggest that you start to think about your tone when you are on the phone, as you have too much else to do. What I would suggest though is that you mean what you say and be confident about why you are calling. Tone will give you away if you're not confident. Your confidence starts with your mind and before you are on the call. Later in this book I will talk about preparation and planning for a cold call. When you get to that part remember what I said here. Think it, believe it, trust in your thinking and the rest will come. Those are the activities which help you to come across as you mean to come across on the phone.

To get through the first door, unlock the fear and stop the chances of rejection:

- Be honest.
- Being FRESH so you can build a good rapport.
- Ask questions so you can stay on the call and qualify the opportunity.
- Keep your opening phrases simple and easy to understand.
- Believe in what you are saying so your tone is read correctly.

DOOR 1: FIRST IMPRESSIONS

HONEST
F.R.E.S.H
RAPPORT
LANGUAGE
TONE

DOOR 2

OBJECTIONS

LOCK 2 – LOSING CONTROL

Objections during cold calling are very common and tend to be one of the main reasons salespeople don't like to make these types of calls. Quite rightly most sales people feel they are gifted in face-to-face interaction, and that phone calls don't allow them to 'shine' in the same way. This is true as we have already said earlier; there are theories which prove the advantages of face-to-face over telephone interactions. However, if there were never any objections on the phone then I can't help think that salespeople would make more cold calls. So let's explore exactly what objections at this stage in the sales process are and how we can overcome or pre-eliminate them:

Objection
NOUN

An expression or feeling of disapproval or opposition; a reason for disagreeing.

Oxford Dictionary (2018)

The Oxford Dictionary also has lots of examples of the word in context and all of them clearly state how the word is about being in opposition. Taking this into account, it's no wonder that salespeople don't like objections. In our minds the word has a negative connotation to it. Hence, our brains which are primitively wired to decide a like or dislike (fight or flight) reaction to an action would feel inclined to want to walk away from (flight)objections rather than face them. Alternatively, where we know we can't walk away or, more likely, 'shouldn't' walk away from it, we tend to fall into a more defensive/conflict (fight) mode or even feel under pressure. Remember, when you are on the phone, these feelings will come across through your tone. For example, as soon as you are asked a question such as "is this a cold call?" the little voice in your head starts "oh no, here we go again, she/he is going to be difficult now, I need to get past this objection", the voice triggers a negative feeling and your body language reflects this. The chest puffs up, or shoulders go down, either way it's not the same posture you had when you started out on the call. The tone then follows the posture and rapport is therefore lost as is control. Believe me it really happens. I watch many salespeople doing this. One might argue that there are other reasons for the way we respond to gatekeepers such as how many calls you have already made so far, how many of the same responses you have had in that day, how tired you are, how well you have succeeded in calls today so far, whether you feel like 'fighting' on this one or just cannot be bothered with difficult gatekeepers. I agree with all these as being real contributing factors though I also believe it can become a vicious cycle. 'Cause and Effect'.[5]

So taking into account that other variables have an effect on how we respond to gatekeepers, we perhaps would do ourselves a favour by eliminating the negativity tied in with the word 'objections'. This will at least take away the thought that you are being challenged. No one needs to feel they are being challenged when doing something that is already out of a comfort zone. Once you can eliminate from your mind that the gatekeeper is challenging you, you start to see their responses as simply questions or statements.

Here are some typical objections you might get during a cold call. These are taken from delegates from training courses I have run, and my own experiences of cold calling for the last 20 years. This may not seem a lot but that's because most are generic to all cold callers.

- Is this a cold call?
- Are they expecting your call?
- What is your call about?
- I can't give any names.
- I can't give you a number.
- I'm not allowed to forward without a name.
- Can you send an email instead?
- Would you like to leave a message, I'll pass it on?
- Where are you calling from?

---

5 **NLP Cause and Effect**. Milton Model pattern.

- Who did you say you are?
- We're not interested in that.
- We don't need any…
- We already have a provider for.
- We don't accept unsolicited calls.
- Not available/busy.

Questions

Is this a cold call?

Are they expecting your call?

What is your call about?

Can you send an email instead?

Where are you calling from?

Who did you say you are?

Would you like to leave a message, I'll pass it on?

Statements

I can't give any names.

I can't give you a number.

I'm not allowed to forward without a name.

We're not interested in that.

We don't need any.

We already have a provider for…

We don't accept unsolicited calls.

Not available/busy.

Now let me simplify this list into categories of responses. Our minds are amazing. They will absorb and believe what you tell yourself and perhaps so far you may have been feeding your brain the wrong thoughts about this list of potential 'responses' from a gatekeeper.

Looking at the lists of questions and statements above there is not one there that is personal and offensive and none that I would say is an expression of disapproval or opposition. So the first thing I would suggest you do is to rename this list as a list of responses rather than objections. If you start to think of them as responses you will find they are easier to reply to. These are generic responses that a gatekeeper probably asks day in and day out depending on their position and how many calls they receive. Just like some salespeople, gatekeepers start to sound repetitive too. So the first thing you have to remember is that,

"It's not personal."

The gatekeeper does not know you so they are not trying to catch you out. Their daily task list probably doesn't include 'humiliate and attack cold callers.' It might say 'field cold calls'. This means they have to be quite strong and impersonal. Yes I know there are some 'jobsworth' gatekeepers out there but very few. Most gatekeepers are good at the job they do because they have good communication skills and can engage in rapport with the right people. So your response can either make or break your rapport with them.

Back to the list and how to respond; looking at the questions in the list, I would imagine you would have a few one-word answers to some of these questions and in some cases you might have more. Remember, how you reply will make or break your chances of building rapport with gatekeeper and hence getting past them and in which case I would advise more than a one-word answer. I would advise the truth as I said earlier in this book; don't be 'an undercover caller', be honest but also add more words. Here's how I would answer the first two for example.

"Is this a cold call?"
"Yes, it is. You must have many of them?
Or
"Are they expecting your call?"
"I'm not exactly sure but I have written to them, are they at their desk now?"

There is a pattern here. Let me explain.

I read an article once written by a sales guru called Mike Weinberg (3) and his words could not have been more perfect in describing what I do with sales questions such as these.

He said you have to think about it like a game of tennis. Every time a gatekeeper throws something at you they are batting a ball toward you. You have a choice at this point as to whether you want to catch the ball or bat it back. If you catch it that's OK at first but then you know another one will be coming at you straight after it and if you catch that one, another will come at you and again and again until you can't catch them anymore and you 'drop the ball' i.e. you're out of the game, or bring it back to the subject, out of the call. You have lost control of the call and you're going to have to put the phone down. The alternative scenario is that you bat the ball back. The ball in this analogy is a question. The best balls are good relevant qualifying questions. So when you look at my responses above to the question I was asked you will see the pattern is that each answer is expanded on with a question back to the gatekeeper. This forms a two-way conversation and hence a greater chance of rapport. The analogy by Mike brilliantly describes what works when handling this type of list of gatekeeper's responses to you.

Let's try it on statements. Here you may not have to answer a question but you will need to still 'bat a ball back' to keep the call alive:

"I can't give any names out."
"OK. If I come back with a name, you will put me through then?"
"We're not interested in that."
"I see. Would that be because you already have a supplier, or am I calling at the wrong time…?"

You see each time I will bat the ball back. As long as I keep batting it back, I am on the phone for longer and the more chance I have of either getting through or qualifying what it will take to get through next time. Try this with each of the lists and add your own.

By following this rule you will find that you gain something from each call. Even if it's just to know what time to call so you can avoid a certain gatekeeper. I've done that one before. Each call you make should be made knowing that you want to gain something from it. The question is, what do you want to gain from each call?

So that brings me to talk about the objective for a cold call.

The first and most important thing you need for cold calling is to know why you are calling. What is your objective? This is all part of preparation. What is the objective for a cold call? Most sales people might say the objective is "to get a sale" others might say "it's to get past the gatekeeper" and some may say "it's to find out more". Like most actions, and behaviours in selling, there are a number of dependencies which will decide which is the better objective for you and because of this you have to make sure that when you set your objective, it is realistic. Being realistic with your own objective can be the difference between being able to keep motivated for longer or to feel like the world is against you on a day like this one.

I remember a cold caller I helped many years ago. This was someone in a call centre and he had worked extremely hard trying to get sales over the phone for a few weeks now. He knew he was being watched by the managers for his lack of results. One of the managers asked me to seek him out and see if I could help him. I'll call him V for the book. V explained to me his situation: a degree graduate desperate to make a success of his sales career that he moved 3 hours away from his family to pursue. He stays in a bedsit and everyday comes in to work with what he and I believe is a great positive attitude and work ethic. He would get on the phone and try really hard to get a sale from each prospect. So I listened to him make a few calls and then asked him what his objective for each call is.

He told me "to make a sale, Shea. I have to make sales because if I don't I know I will be asked to leave and my livelihood depends on this job." So I said to him: "You have the wrong objective." He was surprised and asked me why I would say this as surely that is what he is here for. So I sat next to him and said this: "As long as you are chasing the sale you are not focussing on the person you are speaking to. As long as you are not focussing on the person you are speaking to you are not listening to them. So if you're not listening to them you're not engaging them. Tell me now in that situation would you buy from you?"

He looked at me and said, "So what do I have to do?"

"Engage them into a conversation, listen to them. Then you will relax and then you will get a sale."

He did exactly what I asked him to and sure enough on that day he made two consistent sales and since then whilst in that business consistently sat in the top 5 performers.

He reminded me of this in a long thank you message recently. This was about 12 years after that day.

So the moral of the story is that if you set yourself an objective that is unrealistic you will only put undue pressure on yourself. When this happens your behaviour will change toward being more aggressive or rushed or even disinterested and the consequence of this is that you don't engage with the person on the other end of that phone. At this stage in the sales process that can break your opportunities and your motivation. I have seen behaviours in cold callers that I would say are directly related to their objective. I know when someone is speaking fast or in a pushy way that they are either desperate to achieve their objective to get sales or they are on a time limit so their objective is to make as many calls in the time given. These callers fail to engage. Every time you set an unrealistic objective you will fail it and you will start to show signs of desperation, hence spiral in the wrong direction.

You won't sell anything to a gatekeeper unless they are also the budget holder and decision maker and influencer and any other stakeholder. I have watched and received calls from salespeople who will keep chasing people on the phone and each time their objective is to either 'get through to the decision maker', or to 'sell' to them. Each time they are unsuccessful they put the phone down and then call again. How much time do you think must be wasted by chasing people where you don't even know if there is an opportunity yet? I suppose you might be thinking it's not wasted time because that's exactly why I keep calling, because I don't know what the opportunity is yet so I don't know if I'm wasting my time yet. And if this is what you're thinking then well done you've just realised your real first objective during a cold call:

"Qualify the opportunity."

This objective is realistic and applies to most situations when making a cold call. The best thing about this objective is that when a salesperson focusses on it, and by that I mean feeds their brain that this is what you want to do, your brain will automatically put all your people skills into place and actually enjoy conversations on the phone without any fear of loss of control due to so-called 'objections'. You will actually be able to listen to the person on the other end more intently so you can bat back valuable and relevant questions enough to have a conversation that will determine whether or not this opportunity is worth more effort from you to go to the next level. For you that next level could be an appointment, but the last thing you want to do is go running off to an appointment or sending someone else to meet someone miles away when you don't even know if it's worth the time and travel cost yet. So relax into a conversation and set your mind on finding out what you need to realise the opportunity and where it sits in your pecking order.

Earlier in Door 1 I speak about qualifying questions and I really think it's important that before you start making your calls, that you put together a set of questions that you would like answers for to help you to determine the value of the opportunity.

I also think you should have a second objective in cold calling which comes after you have achieved the first, and whether it takes one call or several these two objectives should be your focus during cold calling:

"Objective 1 – Qualify the opportunity
Objective 2 – Close on the next stage"

The first objective should be the sole focus for you until you know enough to know if this opportunity is worth your time and so how valuable it is for you to close to get to the next stage. Once achieved you can start to focus on the second objective which is about getting to the next level and could be either securing a sale, a next call or face-to-face appointment. The great thing about these objectives is that you are giving yourself a structured approach to a close and also you can come off that call at any time yet still feel that you have achieved something. For example, if the decision maker was unavailable you can still ask the gatekeeper some questions and then note them and appoint to call back. Another probable situation is when the gatekeeper will not be able to answer any of your questions except perhaps about the decision maker's availability. Even that is a step in the right direction. Although, I have to remind you here that what you get from a gatekeeper is down to how well you persist with your questioning.

The second objective should only become relevant and realistic once the first objective has been achieved or exhausted. You could have gathered enough information from the person you are speaking to, to know all you need to pursue further and so at this point you can move your focus onto getting an appointment with the relevant person or decision maker.

CONCLUSION

To get through the second door, unlock the fear and stop the chances of being caught out with objections:

- Know your objective/s.
- Remember there are no objections at this point. They are questions or statements.
- Respond and bat the ball back to them.
- Qualify the opportunity.

DOOR 3

THE DECISION MAKER

LOCK 3 – VERBAL DIARRHOEA

One of the things that always makes me smile is when you see a very good salesperson get past the gatekeeper and then are completely surprised when the person they asked for is suddenly on the other end of the call. It's quite funny to watch because all of a sudden the salesperson starts to talk and words that come out of their mouth are absolutely not what or how they wanted. This is a case of verbal diarrhoea. Overcoming it is not difficult and doesn't require any additional skills other than a little bit of self-discipline and a structured approach.

PLANNING FOR A CALL

The very people that tell me they don't need to plan for a call are the very people who get struck by verbal diarrhoea and it's a shame because these sales people are great before and after this point. How many times would you have done it differently if given the chance to speak to that decision maker again? I know I have been in that position before. I don't now because now:

"I plan therefore I am prepared to win."

So why not take a moment to plan what you do. I'll refer back to our wonderful minds; if you feed your mind with the right information then you will be able to carry out what you have told yourself what you want to do.

YOUR VISION IS YOUR PLAN

There are theories that explain how our brains work. They compute and translate everything in images. This is why the word 'pomme' in France identifies exactly the same thing as the word 'apple' in the UK. The word or noun is not important but its association to the image is. Hence, very young children are taught to speak with pointing actions to associate words with images. Taking this into consideration you will understand now that when you want to do something or carry out an action, your brain has to see or visualise what it is you want to do so that it can then command your muscles into appropriate action. That's why we sometimes refer to goals or aims as a 'vision'. That vision has to be clear for you to achieve it. To ensure you have clarity of vision though a couple of things to consider are that: 1. You have to have the ability to carry out the action. For example, a person who has never learned how to fly a plane is very unlikely to be able to take off in a jet. 2. The situation has to be right, for example you can't open a window in a room where a window does not exist. Some of you may already know this but the reason I am sharing it with you is because it's useful and relevant to know this. When you are selling or want to pick up the phone and sell something you have to believe in your mind that:

1. You can do it, in other words you have the skills, and
2. Your objective is realistic to the situation.

Skills can be taught through self-learning (this book) or through others (training). You also learn everyday through your experiences if you are wise enough to reflect upon them. The second part as I mentioned above is how realistic the objective is. I remember a question on LinkedIn a couple of years ago:

"What are the most important skills for a sales person to be successful?"

As a sales trainer it is a regular question I get asked in person too. My answer is and always has been:

The most important skill for a salesperson to learn is how to plan and set effective objectives. You can be the most skilled person in selling but if you can't feed your brain a clear vision and set out a path to achieve it, you won't know how to put those brilliant skills into effective use.

We have the end in mind, our objectives:

"Objective 1 – Qualify the opportunity
Objective 2 – Close on the next stage"

The plan is how to get there. I wouldn't suggest a script because that takes away the human element and can always be detected. Your path is simply the structure of your call. So you will introduce yourself and your business and briefly explain what you do: 'a value proposition' or strapline. Some call it the 'elevator pitch' because it has to be short, succinct and clear enough to be understood in a short period of time. After which you will qualify the potential and then add value to close to the next stage:

1. Introduce the Value Proposition – This should be slightly tailored to be impactful.
2. Ask questions to qualify – based on what you have researched.
3. Add value and close to the next stage – whatever the next stage is according to their buying process.

VALUE PROPOSITION

To be able to follow the plan you have to be prepared. Being prepared is half the battle and should never be left out or shortcut. I've heard lots of salespeople struggle to explain what they are offering when asked the question on the phone. They fumble about to explain why they are calling and what they can offer because they haven't planned and prepared a basic strapline that is short, sharp, comprehensive and impactful. They use far too many words and end up with as I said verbal diarrhoea. One great tool to have that can avoid this syndrome is a good value proposition. A value proposition is the potential value that your product or service offering can add to their business. By this I mean a really good answer to, why you are taking up their time right now? Anyone in business in today's world might class themselves as busy and so time is valuable to everyone, but mostly to those people you are cold calling. They want to know if what you have to say is of any value to them. Is it worth their time? In other words, we can call this the 'WIFM' (What's in it for me?) and that decision is made on the back of what you say on this call. Having a good value proposition, that rolls off your tongue, is essential for you to come across knowledgeable and confident. As I said earlier confidence is about knowing you are prepared and having something to say that will hit the right mark with this potential customer. Know what you are selling!

Before thinking about what you would say it's probably good to understand that value is a perception and variable elements of your offering will hit the right note with different businesses depending on what they find valuable at that time. For example, if you were looking for a high-speed quality printer due to workload demand and you had a call from someone who says they specialise in cheap printing equipment, it might not appeal to you. In fact, you will probably be led by your perception of the word 'cheap' measured against what you are looking for and hence make a judgement about the company selling to you. Now if you want to hit the right person with the right value proposition you ought to do some homework so you can tailor your proposition to resonate with the decision maker. For example, the same cold caller in the above example could have said: "we are about providing quality printing equipment that is cost effective". That would have probably hit closer to home for you and gained more of your attention. From this simple example you can see how the words you put across in your value proposition are extremely important which means you really ought to find out what's important to your prospect. There are a few ways you might want to do this and again not one way is right or wrong, and a combination is usually required to get the best value proposition.

> *"A good value proposition explains your value add. A great value proposition explains your value add for them!"*

I once had a call from a lady who might have been the best business person in the world but she lost me in the first few minutes. Here's how the conversation went:

> *"Hi, my name's XX calling from XXX and I'm looking to speak to the owner or decision maker of the business."*
> *"Hi, that's me, Shea, how can I help?"*
> *"I wondered if you'd be interested in some sales training."*
> *"Can you explain what you mean a little further?"*
> *"Yes of course we provide sales training and I wondered if you would be interested in our services for your people."*
> *"(Name) did you look us up on our website?"*

"Yes, I believe I did."
"So you know we are a sales training provider?"
"Oh, no, sorry, I must have missed that…"

That just says it all really.

That must have been awful for her because they train sales and she didn't really demonstrate a good sales approach. So my point is that you should see if the company you are calling has a website and explore to find information that will help you to have a mutually beneficial and relevant conversation with the decision maker.

DESK WORK

The website

A good salesperson can spend time looking at a website but a great one will know exactly where to look and for which information:

1. The language – their language will be reflective of who they are and their culture, so terminology they use especially on the home page will be familiar to them, I said earlier refrain from using your own jargon and now I will advise that instead of your own jargon use theirs. This is about mirroring. If you haven't heard of mirroring let me explain; when looking to build rapport with someone you want to try to get into their world, be like-minded so they can see that you are on

the same page. People who are like-minded are more likely to achieve rapport with each other. You become in sync with each other. Many might talk about mirroring in face-to-face situations but it works with any element of communication. Language and words being one of them. The smallest of words can make the subconscious difference between rapport and no rapport. Here's some examples of the types of words you might look out for:

'Bespoke' instead of 'tailored'
'Unrivalled customer service' instead of 'excellent customer service'
'Ideal choice' rather than 'best'
'Primary importance' rather than 'we value first'
'We believe' instead of 'we live in the knowledge'

This list can go on, but as you can see it is everyday language that your prospects have spent time on enhancing and owning so they can make it impactful and reflective of how they want to be perceived. So it would only be respectful and wise to use it with the very people who wrote it. Let me show you how it can work in context to what you might be saying.

Said in your own words:

"I think we can offer you the best service in… which is why I think we can add real value to your business."

Now said using their words:

"We believe we offer an unrivalled level of

service in what we do and this is why I think that we would be an ideal choice to add value to your plans for…"

Both mean the same thing but when you use their words then you will have triggered into their mind some association in words and hence they will be more favourable to you and what you have to say.

2. Promotions – Have a quick look at the news pages or anything on the home page of a website to see if they are keen to shout out about any current focusses. For example, are they shouting about being investors of people, or perhaps they are focussing on other government-driven initiatives such as carbon footprint or environmentally friendly products. Sometimes you will see information on new senior people joining the team and the reasons they are brought on board. This doesn't take long; it's just a quick look at news pages or headlines on the home pages.

3. Commonalities – In the same way as point 2, you can check news pages or front page news on websites to spot people they have worked with, or their current business partnerships. You might have some genuine common connections. If they have worked with someone they are happy to shout about then they probably trust them and have a rapport with them. If you too have worked with that same business that they are shouting about, you can use this to show them that you too are a trustworthy provider. It's like being neighbours or members of a community.

If X has worked with you then we will give you a chance too. The more you can synchronise yourself or get on the same level as the prospect, the more open they will be toward you. So again build it in to your conversation, e.g. "… yes I understand, one of the other reasons I was keen to speak to you is because we share a common connection…"

4. People – Further to making your value proposition relevant to your contact, some company websites have a 'who's who' or a 'our people' page which I find is really useful for getting an understanding of who is responsible for what you are offering. Look through the roles and responsibilities and have an alternative name in case it's not clear or where there might be more than one decision maker be aware that you might not be speaking initially to the main influencer. Hence, when you make an appointment to see them, you might want to ask if there is anyone else who should be in that meeting. Don't be afraid to ask this question. If you are afraid because it might put them off having a meeting with you then you have to question how committed they are to you, and how much your time is worth to you.

"It's not rude to ask, it's wise to seek the answer."

They may say no and that at this stage they would just like to see you themselves. Then that's OK at least you know what to ask when you are at that meeting for the next stages. Note it down!

<u>Social media</u> is another fantastic tool that salespeople today are fortunate enough to have access to:

1. Twitter is great for checking a company's activity. Companies with a presence on this site may have people assigned to promote what they are doing as a business to maintain their presence and promote their successes. You can use this knowledge to build a conversation with your prospect. Something as simple as "oh I saw on Twitter that you are currently working on…" however only mention it if you can make a connection with yourself or what you can offer. Shows how you can support current initiatives don't just praise them for having one. Instagram is another site that people generally post activity on.

2. LinkedIn is a great way to find people and roles they are in. Always good to have a quick check before you call to make sure you have the right person in the right role with the relevant responsibilities for you to sell to. Have a look at what the person/s might have been most recently engaged in as it might be relevant to your value proposition. Also, it might be a good idea to get an alternative name in case your primary contact isn't available.

Research can sometimes highlight or raise some more questions that you can ask your prospect too and these should be noted along with your qualifying questions.

Once the desk work is done, you have to continue your research on the phone. As I already said, your questions are key to moving forward with the right potential customer. You now have to ensure you can control the structure of your call to be able to achieve your objectives. In other words, control the conversation you have with your prospect so you can steer it in the right direction. To steer it effectively whilst having a relaxed conversation you don't just have to be able to ask the questions you would like to ask, you also have to listen to the prospect. If you don't listen you might end up asking all the wrong questions. More importantly, you have to be able to listen enough to understand. Remember to be able to show someone the value you can add will not just be about the homework you did but also about what the person on the other end of this call is saying to you.

Listening

Listening is one of the most important yet probably the least applied skill that salespeople have and even less than planning. I hate to say it but I have put hundreds of salespeople through simulations and watched them in the real world and each time I find almost all of them will spend more time talking than listening. In the past, sales people were spoken about as people with 'the gift of the gab', good at talking. However, the market place is savvy and fast moving. People don't admire that style of selling anymore. My partner Peter and I recently went to a timeshare meeting with my sister's family in Mexico and we had to leave halfway through. The guy just talked at us for about an hour and a half hoping that at some point we would submit to buy thousands of pounds worth of holiday rental. This is old school selling where a salesperson's ability to out-talk everyone else ends up meaning that the buyer will be beaten into submission and give in to whatever it he was selling. I don't believe this helps sales retention though.

Anyway, what I'm saying is have a good value proposition, know what you are saying but remember to have a two-way conversation, but you have to be able to listen.

I don't believe any of us were taught to listen like we were taught to read, write and speak. So perhaps this is the reason why we really don't know what listening is. I've heard many people say and once I believed myself that to be good at listening you have to control your body language, eye contact, and sitting up, nodding. On the phone that would be verbal nods of acknowledgement. Well I'm not quite on board with any of this. I believe that we grew up being *told* to listen but never *taught,* and the words of advice given today for effective listening are simply association words to what we grew up being told. They are simply a more sophisticated way of telling us to be quiet, sit still, face front, as we were told in school. So I train and coach people in a different way. A way which takes into account that we listen primarily with our ears and our minds not our eyes or posture, sure they might help but how many young people today will be tweeting about a match whilst listening to the commentary and be able to repeat the commentary to you afterwards. That's listening. Their brains are engaged with what's being said. How? Well I said earlier how our brains compute information into images, so listening and taking information on board is more about being able to complete a picture in your mind. Think about when you listen to a play on the radio or listen to a conversation where there are no pictures. You will find that to remain engaged with the programme you do it through imagination. You build pictures in your mind of what's being said and how it might look to how the characters might look when a narrator describes them. In the same way you should engage your mind and try to build a picture of what it's like to be in the customer's shoes. I always say;

"It's wise to be in the customer's shoes, not one step ahead of them."

Because what most of us have been guilty of at many points in our lives is to only listen up to a certain point, then our minds can drift. That certain point can be created by a trigger word or phrase. For example, a salesperson might hear the words 'need to review' and jump in with "that's exactly what we can do for you". What can you do for them? They haven't said why they want to review it yet. In selling I've heard salespeople jump in too early during a conversation and end up trying to sell on half an understanding. That's because they are so ready to tell tell tell rather than sell sell sell.

"Telling is not selling."

So how do we avoid the mind wandering off instead of listening and staying with the conversation? Well it's quite simple. Accept the fact that we have the attention span of a gnat and as jumpy as a cat on a hot tin roof, and break the conversation down. The key to good listening is to ask good questions, and then steer the questions by asking more questions based on what the customer just said. Be nosey. Act like you would if a good friend had some juicy gossip to tell you. Reflect on that behaviour. When you are interested in what someone is saying you will be able to use their words to ask them another question. This is how you stay focussed.

Take notes too. Too many salespeople think they can remember everything. Well maybe you can remember most things but when you start working with a structure, plans and preparation, you might find that you are gathering far more information now and that you need to note it down. Once you've written it down it also clears your mind ready for the next call. I can't stress this discipline enough to people. The more you write down now, the better you can plan to close later. You can only feed yourself the information that you note down for yourself. If you note all the things a prospect says are valuable to them, then you can use these to close them later.

Answering machines

I'm sure you will agree that one of the true pet hates for all salespeople is when you've done your homework, are all prepared and successfully charmed your way past the gatekeeper only to be put through to an answering machine. What do you do? Leave a message or not? As I have said before, there is no wrong or right but there is what's best. In my opinion, I would not leave a voice message on an answering machine of a person who does not know me yet. I find that sales people who do this tend to be ticking a box that says they've contacted that prospect. Hmm, not quite. Contact should only be counted when you have a two-way conversation with a human being. I can only imagine that by leaving a voice message with a decision maker that your objective must have been to 'tell the decision maker why you are calling' and not 'to qualify and get an appointment'. By leaving a message without first speaking to the person you have just thrown away all the preparation work and handed over control of your relationship to the machine. I say the machine because there are no guarantees that the owner of that machine will listen to the message fully or at all. Also because the machine might not have a personalised greeting recorded on it, hence you could be leaving a message with completely the wrong person.

By leaving a message you've just given them the heads up on why you are calling so they can make a decision on something which they haven't fully understood or on you by the tone or your words, or simply choose not to call you back. There is a chance that they might call you back but those chances by experience I would say are pretty slim. Oh and now that they have your name, next time the gatekeeper asks them if they want to take your call, you might just get an answer along the lines of "got message thanks, not interested". You just have to ask yourself if this has ever worked for you. Having said all this there might be the odd occasion where a voice message is needed to bring someone's attention to the fact that you are not to be ignored. You are a salesperson, and everyone has salespeople who deserve respect for even picking up the phone.

I had an experience a few years ago where I made a cold call to a sales director, in a fairly senior position. Once through to him and after I introduced myself, he asked me if he could call me back later after his meeting. I agreed but said that I would call him and asked him what time he would be out of his meeting. He told me 5pm. So that was agreed. When I called back, sure enough he answered but as soon as I had said my name he hung up. This was on his mobile by the way. So I called again and he hung up again this time sooner. So I gave it a few minutes and then called again, this time he didn't pick up and it went through to voice mail. Great I thought, so I left a message because now it was needed. My message:

"Hi, X it's Shea, I just have to tell you that in all my years of selling I have never come across a salesperson in a senior position such as yourself to behave in the way you have toward me today. I would have thought you of all people would appreciate cold callers and I really hope that your salespeople do not have to encounter the behaviour I did from you."

This was now just after 5.30pm. Needless to say, I don't think he listened to the message straight away, but he did listen to it that night because the very next morning at about 8am I had a call from this Sales Director apologising for his behaviour and we went on to have a great conversation and I was able to qualify the opportunity.

So there are situations or circumstances that might lead to you leave a voice message but I wouldn't suggest it until you have spoken to them in person first.

The experience I have shared above also covers another part point I want to make which is about closing. I want to talk about that separately as it is relevant in all three doors. So first let's conclude Door 3.

CONCLUSION

To get through the third door, to unlock the fear and stop the chances of verbal diarrhoea:

- Have a vision: a plan with objectives.
- Prepare to win – value proposition (VP).
- Use questions to listen and understand.
- Close to progress to the next stage.

CLOSING ON THE PHONE

Closing is one of those things that many salespeople ask me about and I have to say that to close effectively you simply have to do all of the above and the close will become easier. I remember once I was painting my garden fence and this is a very long fence made up of tight 8-inch wooden fencing boards. I had to do it plank by plank to get good coverage and an even coat. After painting just ten boards I stopped to look at how many I had left to do.

I wish I hadn't because by seeing that I still had lots to do, the job became harder, now I could have started to panic and rush. Instead I took a break and spoke to myself. "I know what I am working to achieve (objective), I have all the tools and enough paint and have found the most effective way to get coverage (preparation) that vision is clear, but to make sure I don't have to go over it again I have to make sure I check each board is completely covered before moving to the next one (closing at each stage), that way I will have the desired finish. If I rush across each board because I feel I have to get to the end, then the end result will have flaws in it; enough to make me have to do it again."

This is like selling. First have your vision clear, this is your objective, and then work on each door at a time, closing each one as you go along, then you will automatically close on your objective.

The Door to the next stage	The Lock (fear)	The Close (the commitment)
1. First Impressions	Fear of rejection	They like you.
2. Objections	Losing control	They help you to qualify and get through to the right person.
3. The Decision maker	Verbal diarrhoea	They will move to the next stage.

"Closing is not just a skill it's an attitude."

If we define close it means to get an agreement or a commitment to something or someone. This can be achieved through both rapport and maintaining control of your fears. To do those you need good communication skills and a strong positive attitude. You do need both though, one without the other just doesn't work. I've heard many a salesperson go in with all guns a blazing, confidence at sky level, talking at their prospects but not really making the effort to build rapport then wondering why they can't close. Likewise, if you are great at building rapport but lack the confidence to ask the closing question, then again, you won't achieve the objective. People buy from people they like, and people they trust.

I have already spoken about the skill in being able to set realistic objectives and planning well. Whilst these may not be during the call they will still play a large part in your ability to close.

Our 3 doors are the stages of the call and at each stage there is a need to close.

To achieve the close at each door you will need to win over the person through your communication skills. If you are liked or create a good impression on the other person then it is more likely that the other person will engage with you for longer, answer more questions, and genuinely help you to achieve your objective. I'm sure if you were to look back at your own choices in buying, you will have preferred to buy from someone who came across as FRESH.

It's very unlikely that you will buy from someone unless they demonstrate good rapport building skills. Remember the line from the movie Pretty Woman "Big Mistake". Julia Roberts's character walked into a store arms laden with shopping bags containing probably thousands of dollars' worth of purchases from other stores. Her line was delivered to a commission based sales assistant and her aim was to emphasise the amount of commission that the sales assistant missed out on by being rude to Julia's character on a previous visit. In large expensive stores you may have in the past experienced an air of arrogance from the sales staff. Would you buy from them?

Trust is essential. I have explained how important it is to be honest and transparent about why you are calling so that people don't put up defences or have to second guess you. Again, trust is also achieved through effective application of communication skills. I think we can all agree that when you speak to someone and need to make a judgement on them, one of the questions you might ask your self is "can I trust this person".

We all like to be treated with respect. Now respect is where we cross into attitude.

ATTITUDE FOR CLOSING

Attitude in selling is made up of a number of internal influencers and cannot really be trained or taught. What I can do though is help you to identify what constitutes the right attitude so you can measure your own:

- Your beliefs: the ability to focus, self-discipline and motivation.
- Your values: loyalty, respect and self-worth.
- Your confidence: ability to ask for the close.

YOUR BELIEFS

This is about, well, you sticking to what you said you would do. That includes being well prepared; your research and planning and setting realistic objectives. Know why you are calling, make notes straight away, and make follow-up calls and emails as promised. Diarise and set reminders when you need to. Don't rely on just your memory. Many a close is lost because people either don't follow up or forget some details that might have been essential to the close. Both these can be avoided by notes and diarising. Many salespeople say they remember to follow up every call but how do you know if you don't have it noted somewhere? If there's no note, there's no measure. Sometimes and especially in some sales roles it's all about being there at the right time. In which case do you really want to risk losing a prospect because you weren't disciplined enough to follow through as promised? Some might call this being lazy, but I think it's more about finding your own way of being organised. You might prefer to use paper diaries or electronic ones; I don't think it should matter which you use, so long as, firstly, you use one and, secondly, you are not duplicating workload. This can be off putting. If you work in a business where you are required to put notes on a system, you might find that it's more time effective to just write everything straight onto the system rather than in your diary first. If you write it in your diary first and then transfer onto the system that can be enough to make you think that note making is wasting your time, and hence you might be inclined to take shortcuts in your notes. If you take shortcuts you might find you are the only one who suffers as a result of that.

Remember why you are doing what you are doing too. Making cold calls one after the other each day is a tough job. So as I mentioned before, keep things around you which remind you why you are making them. One big tip I can give you here is remember to have fun whilst making them. Go into it thinking about the weird and wonderful people you might come across on the other end of that call. My colleagues and managers always used to think I was talking to someone I knew on the phone, because I had fun with them as well as achieving my objective.

VALUES

Cold callers are not given the high level of respect that they deserve and this can be evident in some gatekeepers' and decision makers' behaviour toward cold callers. It's a very inaccurate perception but is the very reason I guess many account managers in sales or business owners don't like to make cold calls. This preconception can make you feel small and it's very hard to stay motivated and focussed when people are rude or ignorant toward you numerous times a day. So this is why your self-worth has to kick in. Believe in who you are and why you are calling.

I have always remained adamant that I shouldn't need to mention my status in my company when I make a cold call because it should not be the reason I get through to the decision maker. I was especially very conscious of this when I made my first few videos on YouTube. I want to show salespeople that you don't have to have a title to get through the door, you just need to do everything I have already said in this book and the other thing is to assume the position.

Part of being prepared is being mentally prepared and this is really about believing in yourself as a professional who has every right to be making the calls that you make. Be proud of what you are doing and own it. Every successful company in the world has had to pick up the phone and sell at one point. Every entrepreneur has made a cold call and some still do. You should never apologise for making a cold call but respect the challenge, prepare your mind so that you don't come across subservient on the phone but more on an equal level to the person you want to speak to. If in your mind you are walking in those shoes then your communication will reflect it. So walk the talk, remember you might be a cold caller but you are also a professional who works hard and has the right to be heard. In the same way, be bold about asking the questions that are right during your conversation. Yes, there are many ways to skin a cat so trust in your rapport building skills and ask away. If you don't ask, you don't get.

On my YouTube cold calling videos you will see how I persist on asking questions and how they just seem to answer them. It's like, the more I ask the more I learn. Subscribers have asked me how I manage to have such a relaxed conversation with people. That's because other than everything else I have suggested in this book, I also prepare my mind by remembering that when you strip all the fancy suits and titles away, you have two human beings who want to simply do a job well. Be on the same level. If it helps, remember that the person you are speaking to has to eat, shit and sleep just the same as you. They live in the same world and walk on two legs just like you. Why should you be scared to talk to them? They are no different or better than you.

Controlling your conversation is a must at all points of the sales process and it starts right here on your first call.

Sometimes you might catch a decision maker on their way into a meeting or they simply ask you if they can call you back. If you want to maintain control of the opportunity I would suggest you always take ownership of calling them back. Another scenario might be that at the end of a call you might find the person you just spoke to asks you to leave it with them as they have to discuss your proposition with someone else. That's fine but I would make sure you find out when they will be speaking to that person and hence when you should call them back. We've all heard of the 'I'll call you, don't call me' cliché. Well make sure you turn that around and maintain control of contact. How many times have you put the phone down and then had to start to chase all over again? It's like taking two steps forward and one backwards. So make it easier on yourself. Ask them to agree with you now when the next contact should be and hold them to it. In my words:

> *"Great, so I'll call you back but when will be the best time to call you so I don't end up missing you?*
> *"Which number shall I call you on?"*
> *"Which number is best to get you on?"*
> *"Can I call you on your mobile or direct line next time?"*

None of the above questions are harmful but they are strong and will set you up for the next call. Just remember you don't want to have to start again, if you have to call back you will but the next one should be easier.

Another part of keeping control is when a prospect agrees to a meeting and then tells you they will email you some dates! I've witnessed this one before when coaching salespeople but I've also had prospects say this to me. My response:

"Well have you got your diary there with you?"

Of course they have, they're in the office. The only time I won't use this response to that statement is when the prospect is driving in which case I will say:

"When are you next with your diary? I'll call you then unless I hear from you beforehand."

Now some of you might be thinking, wow that's a bit hard or direct or strong. Well it is only any of those things if you haven't built the right level of rapport with the person. This is why I say you have to have both skill and attitude.

Another scenario might be when a prospect tells you that they need to speak to someone else:

"OK, who else would need to be a part of this?" Actually you may have tried to qualify this earlier but sometimes prospects like anyone are a little protective of their position and like to feel they have more authority to buy than they let on. The good news about this kind of response is that they now actually think you are worth talking about to their seniors or peers.

So your response should be to find out who it is and offer to come and meet with everyone. This is a great opportunity to close on a meeting or the next stage. Remember you are on that call to achieve something. So make sure you ask for it!

Provided you have applied your skills effectively and maintained control throughout, then most responses from the prospect at this stage will invite you to close on your objective. Seize the opportunity while it's hot!

CLOSING AT EACH DOOR

At Door 1 – Make the right first impression. Your close is to be liked. Remember the importance of being liked at this stage. Gatekeepers won't entertain you or your questions if they just don't get a good first impression of you. So as I said, use the skills and have a confident attitude.

At Door 2 – Maintain control. Your close is to gain commitment from the gatekeeper to help you qualify and get you through to the right person.

At Door 3 – Show them the value in speaking to you further and gain commitment to move forward. This could be a meeting, demo, call or whatever your next stage in your sales process is. Ask for the next stage.

Key points to close effectively:

- Have an objective and follow a plan at each stage.
- Ask enough questions so you know when to close at each stage.
- Ask for commitment at each stage of the process to move to the next.
- Maintain control throughout.
- Maintain rapport throughout.
- Don't be afraid to Ask!

SUMMARY

I am a great believer in letting salespeople be themselves because the fact that you have chosen to be in sales or anyone has hired you to be in sales, means that you probably already have some of the raw natural attributes required to do the job. Someone saw something in you that told them you can do it. If you are struggling then perhaps you haven't yet told yourself that you have what it takes, or perhaps you are trying to improve your success rate by cloning others' behaviours. What you might need is a little help in being more self-aware of how your approaches and behaviour might impact on your prospects. My book's aim was to help you with that. Along the way I have shared with you some stories that you might be able to identify with and some that might reassure you that you are not the only person who might have thought that way. In some cases, the book might have simply confirmed for you what you already know works well for you. The idea was to help you to self-analyse your cold calling and then help you to think about how you might change some of your behaviours, habits and approaches so you can achieve a greater success rate from your calls. Don't try to be someone else. Be you, but be a better you.

> *"Being a good salesperson requires skills. Being a great salesperson requires an attitude to improve."*

REFERENCES

(1) Albert Mehrabian – Mehrabian, A. (1981). *Silent messages: implicit communication of emotions and attitudes* (2nd ed.). Belmont, Calif.: Wadsworth Pub. Co.

(2) Transactional analysis – *Transactional analysis in psychotherapy*. Volume 386 of A black cat book. Author, Eric Berne. Publisher, Grove Press, 1975. Original from, Pennsylvania State University. Digitized: May 3, 2011. ISBN, 0394172299, 9780394172293. Length: 298 pages.

(3) Mike Weinberg – *The Closer* online Sales Publication Magazine – Now offline.